CHURCHGOING FOR AMATEURS

Churchgoing for Amateurs

Michael Green

Hodder & Stoughton
LONDON   SYDNEY   AUCKLAND

Copyright © 2000 Michael Green
Illustrations copyright © 2000 by Taffy Davies

First published in Great Britain in 2000

The right of Michael Green to be identified as the Author of
the Work has been asserted by him in accordance with
the Copyright, Designs and Patents Act 1988.

10 9 8 7 6 5 4 3 2 1

British Library Cataloguing in Publication Data
A record for this book is available from the British Library

ISBN 0 340 74605 X

Typeset by Avon Dataset Ltd, Bidford-on-Avon, Warks

Printed and bound in Great Britain by
Clays Ltd, St Ives plc

Hodder and Stoughton Ltd
A Division of Hodder Headline
338 Euston Road
London NW1 3BH

Contents

Church? Not for me, thanks!

It's a remarkable thing, but churchgoing has become one of the most despised of all activities in the Western world. Remarkable, because Western civilisation was very largely built upon the Christian faith and the church which propagated it.

Not so today.

Less than 6 per cent of people in Britain go to church regularly, although most people claim to pray quite often, and spirituality of all kinds is a massive growth industry. New Age stores proliferate, mystic channellers are in, near-death experiences are fashionable, Buddhism is chic and Eastern meditation is financed by some companies for their employees. But church? No thanks!

Perhaps that is not altogether surprising, for as Daniel Defoe observed long ago,

> Whenever God erects a house of prayer,
> The devil always builds a chapel there;

And 'twill be found, upon examination,
The latter has the largest congregation.

Nevertheless, until the early part of this century most people went to church. It was part of Sunday. Even ardent unbelievers would go to church on wheels – in a pram when they were baptised, in a carriage when they were married, and in a hearse when they were buried. Now even that has changed. Fewer and fewer children are baptised, marriages take place anywhere, and humanists are devising funeral services for unbelievers.

So if you invite your neighbour to church, the answer you are most likely to get is a polite – or not so polite – 'Church? Not for me, thanks!' Why this intense and almost universal distaste? Why this massive cultural about-turn within two or three generations? It is very understandable. There are good reasons. Read on!

Part One

The church as it often appears

1

Church? It is culturally alien

I saw a remarkable advertisement the other night on the TV. A Dr Geoffrey Clements was giving a party political broadcast on behalf of the Natural Law Party. You have never heard of it? Neither had I. But here they were taking adverts on all the television channels. They must have put loads of money into it. And what was their programme? Yogic flying, no less! The idea is that if enough people engage in yogic flying it will produce peace waves countrywide, which will eventually affect the whole world. These waves will radiate through the environment like sound waves. Seven thousand yogic flyers will produce peace throughout Europe. They will create a stable cultural consciousness which will cut crime and enable everyone to develop their full potential. Wars will end and peace will reign. This is the hope, the only hope, for peace, harmony and happiness in our time.

Presumably people believe that rubbish. Some of them

join the Natural Law Party. They will buy into space invaders from Mars, into *Star Wars*, into yogic flying, even though these things are highly imaginative and have no basis in fact. There is plenty of credulity around these days. Spirituality is a must for people who know what's what. But will they even dream of going to church? Not on your life. Such a thing would not cross their minds. It is culturally alien – in a way yogic flyers are not!

And yet Christianity is one of the most powerful foundations on which our whole culture is built. There was a unified church in Britain long before there was a unified state. That is why the Archbishop of Canterbury crowns the king or queen. But today the church seems old hat.

Why should this be? That is a very good question, because Christianity is growing worldwide faster than it has ever done. Why should we regard it as so alien to *our* culture, our way of living here in Britain?

Well, it's out of fashion. That's the truth of it. Most people simply don't go to church. It isn't cool. And it hasn't been for two or even three generations. The result? Vast numbers of people in our country have not the foggiest idea of what Christianity is about. And they have never in their lives been inside a Christian church.

But that only pushes the question further back. Why is it so unfashionable? Why has the mass of people turned against it, or simply never given it a thought? There are lots of reasons, and some of them are impressive.

6

For one thing, most churches are very strange places if you are not used to them. There is an ancient church in the Romney Marshes of Kent where this sign hangs in the porch, 'Keep door firmly shut. Sheep may enter.' This has been, for many years, the unspoken message of many churches: 'This church is not your scene. Keep out.' Of course they would never put it like that, but that's the impression people get. After all, no concessions are made for newcomers, nor much of a welcome. In liturgical churches you are left to sink or swim so far as knowing where you are in the service. Why, you are often landed with three books as you come through the door – and in a non-reading culture! What's more, you have a largely silent part to play. You stand up, sit down, kneel, perhaps receive communion, put your money in the plate. The only vocal contribution you are expected to make is to sing hymns! Very strange.

But of course it goes far deeper than that. A silent revolution has been going on in our civilisation during the past forty years or so. It marks a decisive break with the way of looking at things which has prevailed for two hundred years and more. You recall the sort of thing: education and upbringing placed a big emphasis on the intellect, on logical argument, book-learning, generally accepted morals and customs, respect for institutions, your elders and betters and so on. Not much of that these days! Feelings matter more than books – and you are not likely to get exciting feelings in most churches! We do not like belonging to institutions – they fetter our freedom. And the church is one of those institutions. We

do not like authority figures very much – nobody is going to tell me what to do! Undeniably the church is a hierarchical institution with clergy as authority figures. Keep well away.

Anyway, the world is a global village nowadays, with people from a variety of nationalities thronging our streets; surely their religion, if they have one, is just as good as Christianity? To be sure, the church teaches that God has revealed himself – but how can you believe in revelation when the discoveries of science have shown us all we need to know? There are no absolute standards of right and wrong, of truth and falsehood. What is right for me may not be right for you. What's true for me may not be for you. It's all relative. Up to the individual. Take your pick.

That's the climate, isn't it? And if morals are a matter of choice, and if the Christian faith appears much the same as other religions, why bother about that fuddy-duddy old institution, the church? The buildings are uninviting. It is, in any case, so old-fashioned. They wear funny robes from hundreds of years ago. The services in most of them are just as old – though some of them, by way of contrast, make a pathetic attempt to be contemporary and 'with it'. Churchgoing may be OK, perhaps, for little children and the very old, but it has nothing to offer red-blooded men and women in today's culture.

Most of all, we are accustomed to having masses of choice. Choice in the supermarket, choice in our entertainments. And the church is not very entertaining.

There are so many other things to do on a Sunday that are much more fun than going into an antiquated building, singing old hymns (or sentimental modern choruses), praying to a God who may exist but doesn't seem to do anything for us, and listening to someone preach away for twenty minutes. No thanks, that's not my scene. It's culturally alien.

Yes, I understand just how you feel. I often feel that way too, when I go into some particularly dreary church. But the existence of dud ten pound notes (or churches) does not rule out the value of real ones. Churchgoing doesn't seem culturally alien when Princess Diana dies, or when you want to get married. Anyhow, real Christianity is and has always been counter-cultural. It is God's invasion, God's revolutionary movement among a bunch of human rebels. No wonder it seems a bit alien to begin with. It felt alien in the Roman Empire, when Christianity first began. But it captured that empire. It felt alien in Europe when fierce pagan tribes roamed the continent. But it captured Europe, too. It was the same in Africa. Think how alien Christianity was to Africans when people like David Livingstone were pioneers for the gospel in the middle of the nineteenth century. Culturally alien to start with, but think how massive a movement Christianity is in Africa today.

The church has a nasty habit of making a comeback just when you think you have finally got rid of it! That happened with a vengeance in Stalin's Russia and Mao's China in our own lifetime. It happened in the eighteenth

10

century when the spiritual revival led by Wesley and Whitefield changed the whole religious and moral face of Britain, within fifty years. It could happen again even in today's culture, where it seems so alien!

2

Church? It is personally irrelevant

'I don't mind going to church for a wedding, especially if the bride is good looking. I don't mind even going to a funeral, though I am keen to get out of the spooky place and have a cigarette. But church as a regular thing? You must be joking. It's not my scene.'

Haven't you had something like that said to you by a friend, if you are a churchgoer? And if you pursue the matter, and try to find out why your friend is so resistant to church, you will probably get a very short answer! But just possibly they might take the trouble to tell you why they have no use for the church. They might even lay it out for you in a clear and orderly fashion, so that you never bring up the subject again. It could well amount to something like this.

'First and foremost, *it is simply not done* to go to church. It's as basic as that. Naturally we are all enormously influenced by our surroundings, by our friends, and by what is socially accepted – even in an age of doing your

own thing. Well, it is definitely not cool to go to church. People don't do it. Of course there are some that like that sort of thing, mostly elderly women and young children. But in most Western countries these days I think you will find more than 90 per cent of the population keeping well away from church on a Sunday, and you can make that 95 per cent for young people. If I am going to buck the trend, then I need a good reason for doing so.

'Then again, as far as I'm concerned, *it is irrelevant*. I mean, what reason could there be for me to go to church? That's not just a problem I have. It is clearly what many churchgoers think. Haven't you noticed the trend for real church enthusiasts to drop from going twice a Sunday to once? Haven't you noticed that the regulars are now much less regular – they go away for many of the Sundays of the year? Even the Roman Catholic Church, which has hitherto been the most successful in holding its members, is now facing a massive fall-out of churchgoers, and half the Catholic churches in the world are short of a priest? No, even the church people find they can very easily do without it. It does not scratch them where they itch. In any case, what is the fun in going week by week for an hour into a half-empty mediaeval building, with its own musty smell, its uncomfortable seating, and its lack of action?

'Actually, that leads naturally into another good reason why I do not go. *Church is so boring*. If you do a rough survey among the young people you know, that is the main complaint. It is not that they do not believe in God or Jesus – many of them do. But they see no reason why they should be bored stiff on a Sunday, when life is full of far more interesting things to do. I agree with them. Maybe churchgoing was acceptable for many people when they had nothing else to do on a Sunday, and all the pubs and shops were shut. But we are a far cry from that today. I want to get out there and enjoy myself. But I didn't find much joy or even much welcome when I gave church a try.

'Don't mistake me. It is not that I am leaving out *the spiritual aspect* of life. People have made that mistake for a century and more, thinking that science and technology would solve all our problems and give us inner peace as well as external prosperity. Many of us these days see the barrenness of that approach. Please understand that I and my friends do have a spirituality, but we are not looking towards the church to fulfil it, because we frankly doubt whether the church has much in the way of spirituality. It always seems to go on about whether women and homosexuals should be priests, whether to play sport on Sunday, and whether to use the old Prayer Book or the revised one – and I hear they are going to revise it again! How irrelevant can you get? I get my spirituality looking at a glorious sunset, walking with my girlfriend barefoot along the beach at night, cycling in the mountains, listening to channellers or people who have had near-death experiences. I really would not dream of looking for spirituality in church.'

Those are the sort of points your friend might well make. It all adds up to a serious indictment.

Churchgoing is not a normal part of modern Western culture. It seems irrelevant to most people. It does not engage their emotions and involvement – it is boring and dull. And it fails to meet the hunger for spirituality which is one of the unsuspected features of our age. Those are widely held perceptions. How might we begin to respond to them?

Christianity may seem to be in decline, some would say terminal decline, in the West. But worldwide it is growing at the rate of between 70,000 and 90,000 new believers every day. And the majority of these come from the countries which have rigorously attempted to stamp out Christianity altogether. I think of Russia and China in particular. Both are experiencing a massive Christian revival. When the missionaries were kicked out of China in 1950 there were perhaps a million Christians in the country. Now the government itself reckons that there are more than 75 million, and rising. Not bad for a Christianity in terminal decline, eh? Much the same is true not only of Russia but of most of the countries in Eastern Europe, that suffered under communistic atheism. Albania was so fierce in its persecution of Christians that not one priest was left alive. And yet now the gospel is growing apace in the schools and even in the parliament of Albania. The Bible Society reports astonishing advance in Sudan. So great is the impact of the *Jesus* film, distributed by the Society, that 4.7 million Sudanese have registered their decision for Christ in the past year. Christianity is not cool in the West? Perhaps it is the West which is out of step.

Is Christianity irrelevant to personal life? Let me continue that report from the Sudan: 'Whole families are being changed. Relationships between husbands and wives, children and parents are being restored. We are seeing communities being changed. The change is not only spiritual but in every area of life. It could even become a major factor in finding a solution to the civil war.' To come nearer home, the comedians Cannon and Ball are notable Christian converts from a wild lifestyle. 'We had all the money, all the toys, the women and the drink we could possibly want. They were our gods in life. But inside I was empty,' wrote Bobby Ball. It is not the church that has made that difference to them: it is Christ. But their conversion has put them among the Christian family called the church. They and millions like them find following Jesus far from irrelevant: it is utterly fulfilling and life-changing.

Is church dull? Yes, often it is, if the church and its minister are just playing it by the book without spiritual vitality and imagination. It is dull if it is all a monotone from the front. It is dull if ancient psalms are intoned by a paid choir that doesn't believe a word of them. But there is nothing dull about *Songs of Praise*. There is nothing dull about Holy Trinity, Brompton, where crowds queue to get in. There is nothing dull about a village church I went to recently where the place was packed out. A young man and his father, both new Christians, were being baptised that day amid scenes of great joy. The vicar held a men's meeting in the pub, introduced by a beer-tasting competition. I spoke after that (on 'Taste and see that the Lord is good. Happy is the man who puts his trust in him') and the ensuing lively discussions went on all over the pub long after closing time. They told me that the winsome Christianity coming from the church was transforming village life. No, it is only dead religion that is dull. Real Christianity is all about knowing and loving and serving Jesus – and nobody ever called him dull!

As for spirituality, I agree that many churches lack it. But that is because they are not allowing the Holy Spirit to break into their services and ritual. You only have to look at Christians of the calibre of Mother Teresa or Cardinal Hume to see an immensely attractive spirituality shining through. It attracts all sorts of people who have no Christian beliefs whatever. And that is the normal Christian life. Anything less is subnormal. But the big thing about Christian spirituality compared with New Age, for example, is that you do not have to throw away your brains to get this spiritual experience. The Christian faith is eminently reasonable and it is radically fulfilling. There is no contradiction between belief in God and experience of God. Christian spirituality does not just give you a high from time to time: it permeates and makes sense of the whole of life. It would be a mistake to write off its relevance too cavalierly.

3

Church? It is socially ineffective

There is another downside to the church in many people's eyes. It does not *do* anything. Its members meet on a Sunday to sing hymns, listen to a sermon (or sleep through it!) and perhaps receive Communion. But that seems to be about it. The members of the church are indistinguishable in their ordinary daily lives from the rest of the population. So why bother about church?

That is a good question. If the church really does not do anything apart from meeting to sing hymns, then forget it! But wait a minute. Is the accusation fair?

The Christian church has always seen its purpose as twofold: to worship God and to share in his mission of love to humankind. So meeting for worship is an essential part of the church's existence. It may seem strange to those who are not Christian, but it is the most obvious thing in the world to those who are. They want to meet together, as the New Testament puts it, 'to declare the praises of him who called you out of darkness into his wonderful light'. Extreme language? No. Lovers' language. Once you have experienced the loving touch of God's welcome and forgiveness, you want to thank him with everything you have. Of course, therefore, there will be hymns and psalms and spiritual songs – and maybe dance and incense as well. You want all you have and all you are to show your joy and gratitude to the Lord. You want to express the fact that you are not the most important pebble on the beach: you are a creature extolling the worth (that's what worship means!) of your Creator. A fitting response. So let's stop knocking the hymn singing, shall we?

However, if church was only about worship, that would be dangerously one-sided. The God whom Christians worship is a God of love and gracious care for every one of his creatures. And if we claim to have dealings with him, inevitably something of that loving, generous characteristic of his must rub off on us. There is a powerful piece of logic in one of the smaller letters in the New Testament. 'We love because he first loved us. If anyone says, "I love God," yet hates his brother, he is a liar. For anyone who does not love his brother, whom he has seen, cannot love God, whom he has not seen. And he has given us this command: Whoever loves God must also love his brother' (1 John 4:19–21). I can't argue with that, can you?

That is the basic reason why, wherever the church has been vibrantly alive, it has had a great concern to improve the lot of other human beings. So the church has been the pioneer in education wherever it has spread throughout the world. It has been the pioneer in medicine, too. And in liberation – be it from exploitation (through helping to establish trade unions), from dying in agony (through the founding of hospices) or from slavery itself (through the tireless efforts of Christians like Wilberforce and Newton). And so you could go on. Who cares about the conditions of deep-sea fishermen? The church. Who initiated prison reform? The church. Who initiated compassionate action for abandoned children? The church. Or refugees? Or the starving in Sudan? Or the deaf? Or the prostitutes? Or the relief of Third World debt? In every case you will find that the church has taken the initiative.

Often the church's action has pricked the conscience of a nation. In due course the government has taken the operation over and enlarged it, as has happened with hospitals and schools in many parts of the developing world: they were started by Christians but later taken over by national governments. That is fine. The church has no monopoly of caring. It loves to act as a spur. But let us be very clear that social action in the name of Christ is a fundamental characteristic of the church. Worship of God and ministry to mankind is what the church is all about. If either of those two gets out of balance you have trouble.

There is trouble when the church gets so heavenly minded it is no earthly good. I saw that among some of the Christians in South Africa in the days of apartheid: they felt sorry for oppressed black people but did nothing to change the situation, confident that they

WORSHIP TO GOD

LOVE TO PEOPLE

would have a better deal in heaven! That is not the way of Christ, and it is good to recall that it was the church that played a major part in bringing about the end of apartheid.

There is trouble, too, when the church gets so earthly minded that it ceases to lift people to God. It becomes just another branch of the social services. True Christianity has two arms: one raised up in worship to God and the other reaching out in love to people. Real Christianity is not socially irrelevant. True, there have been terrible failings, because the church is made up of fallible human beings. But the overall social record of the church cannot be paralleled by any other institution. If a church has no social impact, it is not authentically Christian.

Consider, for a moment. If it were possible to remove all the church people from voluntary social organisations in any of our Western lands, those institutions would collapse from lack of support. And there is another truly remarkable fact to be taken into account. Professor Lamin Sammeh pointed it out at the 1998 Lambeth Conference. Wherever Christians have gone and shared the gospel on a 'we mean to stay' basis, in every case it has empowered and renewed the culture. There is not one single documented case of a culture being oppressed by Christians who have gone out there and meant to stay. That applies as much to work in the inner city or among different racial groups in our own country as it does to ministry overseas.

I want to close this chapter by recounting a small but

highly significant example of authentic Christian social involvement. It happened at the Atlanta Olympics. The weather was unbelievably hot, and spectators were in danger of fainting on the streets. I noticed that officialdom was selling bottles of ordinary tap water at two dollars each. But the Salvation Army and Youth With A Mission combined to give it away free! At the same time they were distributing the *Jesus* film within the Olympic Village. A superb combination of the church's twin calling to serve mankind and glorify God.

4

Church? It is hopelessly divided

The churches are hopelessly divided. Any fool can see that. And any fool has a profound hunch that this should not be the case. What is the point of joining an organisation that can't even get its own internal act together? I mean – which of these rival churches is the one to go to? And why? And what is the difference?

The scandal of disunity has been around for nearly a thousand years, since Roman Catholics and the Orthodox Churches split over whether the Holy Spirit came from God the Father alone or from the Father and Jesus! Can you believe it? I'm afraid I can. I have seen churches split over far more frivolous issues. Then there was another massive division five hundred years later, at the Reformation. And the churches of the Reformation then split into thousands of tiny fragments, while the Roman Catholic Church succeeded in keeping its (very real) divisions within the body of the church.

Division and doing one's own thing seems to be

endemic in human nature. It is clearly endemic in the church. But Christians talk about being reconciled to God from whatever background they came. They talk of the one Christian faith and the one Christian church. Why don't they live that way? Their Christianity can't be all that effective if they cannot live in peace with one another. They talk about reconciling people to God. How can we believe a word of it since they are clearly not reconciled with each other? There must be a deep hypocrisy in the Christian scene. At best, it cannot provide the unity it proclaims. Keep well away.

The Christian churches need to take this criticism firmly on board. My experience over forty years is that those outside the church regard its divisions as far more scandalous than those within. The insiders have got used to them: they are comfortable with them, like a favourite suit of well-worn clothes. They give sophisticated theological justification for their continued divisions. And in so doing they blind themselves. They fail to see how shocking these divisions are. They are indeed shocking, sinful demonstrations of the perversity and sheer wickedness which remains in those who become Christians. Denominations are the proof, if any were needed, of the sinfulness of the church.

On the night before his death, at the Last Supper, Jesus offered a profoundly moving prayer to his heavenly Father. It is recorded in John 17. He is praying for his disciples and those who would follow them. He prays particularly for two things: their mission in the world, and their unity. It is clear that the two belong together in his mind. He prayed 'that they might be one, so that the world might believe'. Alas, they have not managed to remain one, and the world has not believed. To put it bluntly, one of the main reasons for the resistance of our society to the Christian faith is the sinful division of its churches.

It was not always like that. In the first days of the church there was a strong temptation to split. Within a very few years a remarkable Christian church sprang up in Samaria, a small country full of passionate opponents of Judaism. The hatred between them had lasted for centuries. Surely these Samaritan believers would form an independent church, out of communion, as they say, with the Jewish Christians of Judaea? But no. They refused to go that route. There was a marvellous reconciliation, and the one church of Christ embraced Jewish and Samaritan Christians without differentiation. It truly amazed people. It embodied the reconciliation the Christians proclaimed. Read all about it in Acts 8. But then read on a couple of chapters, and you will find another strong temptation, which the early Christians managed to resist. Cornelius was a Roman army officer who was converted along with his extended household. Were they acceptable just as they were? Or would they have to go through all the paraphernalia of becoming Jews – food laws, circumcision, Sabbath-keeping and the rest? You can imagine what a meal modern ecclesiastical bodies would make of something like that. But the first Christians were clear. Jesus had called them to be one body, and they were determined to obey. So they maintained the unity of the church, Jewish, Samaritan and Gentile, and they brushed aside the man-made obstacles which stood in the way.

As a result that united church captured the mighty Roman Empire. Its message of one God, one way of salvation through Jesus, one life-changing Holy Spirit, one family embracing all colours and backgrounds and social classes – why, it spread like wildfire. You could persecute these Christians, but they held together and if necessary died together. You could throw them to the wild beasts but they perished rejoicing in the privilege of suffering for their Lord. No wonder the Roman Empire in due course surrendered to their Jesus. Without the unity of the church it could never have happened.

There you have it. Modern disunity makes no impact on society. Ancient unity made massive progress for the gospel. Will we never learn?

And will we never repent? There is still not much sign of repentance among Christians for their appalling divisions. Instead, different churchmanships and denominations major on their special emphases. Implicitly or explicitly they delight to unchurch one another. Jesus must weep to see such behaviour.

However, all is not bleak. Attempts were made early in the twentieth century through the World Council of Churches to pull the different churches together (on a minimal credal basis, it has to be said). These largely fell apart. But as soon as they did so a movement of 'churches together' began to emerge all over Britain. This was grass-roots stuff. Christians realised that the things which they held in common were much more significant than those which separated them, and they began to meet together, pray together, evangelise together and engage in joint social action.

It often falls to me to lead evangelistic events in different parts of the country. I practically never do it for one church alone or one denomination alone. It is almost always across the board, from Roman Catholics to house churches. That is a very encouraging development in recent years. It would have been unthinkable twenty years ago. But now Protestants no longer regard all Roman Catholics as 'unsaved'. Roman Catholics no longer regard all non-Romans as 'outside the church'.

Did I hear you mutter 'Northern Ireland'? Very well. Let's take Northern Ireland, as an example. I wonder if you have any idea how closely real Christians among the Catholic and Protestant communities are working together, for integrated housing and schooling, in shared prayer and worship, in love and caring for one another? That is not what you hear on the news, where the hard-line men of violence take centre stage. But that is what you find on the ground. I have met a number of men who have spent long years of bitter frustration and hatred in the Mays Prison, until they have come to the point of entrusting their lives to Christ. Catholics and Protestants, who have moved from traditional tribal groupings to life-changing encounter with Christ, have found his love flowing into them and through them to their traditional enemies. You can imagine the amazement that has caused.

The fact of the matter is that those who are not merely formal members of the church but are committed followers of Jesus already have a profound unity, forged by God's indwelling Holy Spirit. It may not be echoed yet in the formal church affiliations to which they belong, but it is there, and they are well aware that the things which divide are as nothing compared with the treasures in Christ which they share together.

And what are the things that divide? Curiously enough, it is not divergence over a whole mass of Christian teaching. Far from it. When you look into it, you will find it centres on two things. One is the precise meaning of the two sacraments of baptism and Holy Communion. And the other is the shape of leadership in the Christian community. Almost all church division centres round these two issues. It is pathetic. There is agreement about God the holy Trinity, about the person and work of Jesus, his incarnation, death and resurrection. Agreement about the Bible, as the foundation of Christian belief and behaviour. Agreement about the function of the church, to worship God and reach out to humankind. Agreement on the whole spectrum of Christian teaching, apart from the sacraments and church leadership. We have got a great deal to be ashamed of. And those who say 'Church? It's hopelessly divided' are absolutely right to draw attention to the scandal of division. What they may have missed out on is the vast solid core of Christian teaching and lifestyle which all churches affirm. But if that is to become evident, visible union must remain a top priority for the churches. Only then will your average punter believe they have got something which everyone needs.

Part Two

The church as God meant it to be

5

The church Jesus prayed for

Have you ever wondered if the church is a great mistake? How is it that Jesus came preaching all about the kingdom of God – and what emerged was the church? Well, that is true, but only half the truth. Jesus said nothing about the church as an institution. It is questionable whether he ever thought of it in those terms. But what is very clear is that he did not rest content with individual religion. When people committed themselves to him they found themselves, willy-nilly, in a community. He called it on one occasion his 'little flock'. There was a sense of belonging.

How right they are to say that Christianity which does not begin with the individual, does not begin. Yes, but Christianity which ends with the individual ends. As soon as you go through the gate of repentance for the past, and put your trust in Jesus as your Lord and your Saviour, you find yourself part of a joyful, jostling crowd.

That is very obvious in the Gospels. Jesus is rarely to be found on his own. He goes around all the time with a group of friends who watch him, help him and learn from him. He calls them his disciples, his learners. And he certainly thought that group would continue. It would be a sort of embodiment of what life in the kingdom of God might look like. Indeed, it would be an agency for bringing the kingdom into many lives and into the structures of society. This was the community he brought into being. He led it. He expected it to continue after his death. It did, and today it represents the largest faith in the world.

What did Jesus want to see in his church? Well, we are not left in ignorance of that. In Jesus' great prayer at the Last Supper, recorded as it is for us in John 17, he reveals his expectations for his 'little flock'. He gives a number of characteristics of the church he was leaving behind to continue his work. They make up a perfectly astonishing list.

First and foremost, we read, the church consists of people who 'know God and Jesus whom he has sent' (verse 3). Not just know about him, you notice, but *know* him. Christianity is all about relationship with Christ.

Moreover, the church is made up of people who set out to 'glorify' Jesus, just as he glorifies his heavenly Father (verses 4 and 5). It's a deep word, glorify. It's all to do with light. And it means letting the sheer weight of God's radiance be reflected in the way you live. Just as the moon reflects the glory of the sun, Christian people are meant to reflect the glory of the Lord, so that people can look at them and say 'There's something different about those folk.'

The church consists of people who 'keep his word' (verse 6). By this Jesus means that those who observe his teaching, revere it, and try to obey it, rather than find ways of circumventing its challenge.

The church consists of people who genuinely believe that Jesus came from God and that God sent him for his unique mission (verse 8). He was not only a great teacher, but God's chosen emissary. Christians are intended to have clear views about the divine origin of Jesus.

The church consists of people who share something of the joy which marked Jesus himself (verse 13). That is perfectly compatible with sorrow and loneliness at times. But it is the governing emotion of the Christian life. Why not, if Christ loves them and died for them? It can't be all bad if that is the case, can it? Christians have something to sing about.

The church consists of people who live their ordinary lives in the world, but are sustained by God (verses 14–18). They are not hermits, taken out of the world. Nor are they worldlings, submerged in it. They are just ordinary people displaying in their way of life the extraordinary power and love and holiness of God.

The church consists of people who can face the music (verse 14). People who will stick to their guns even when the going is rough. The world may well hate them, just as it hated Jesus. They are called to endure, as he endured. That is one of the marks of the true church of God, and we see it manifested today in places like the Sudan, China, and Muslim lands where the church is under constant pressure and often active persecution.

The church consists of people whose home and priorities are not bounded by this world (verse 16). They are, in a sense, aliens and exiles here, as Jesus was. That does not mean they will not throw all their weight into changing and improving society. They will. But they know that this world is not all there is. It is not their final home.

The church consists of people who do not sit comfortably in a Sunday service and then wait for a repeat performance next week. They see themselves as sent out into the world, as Jesus was sent by his heavenly Father, to bring God's love and healing to needy people (verse 18). Jesus' great purpose is that others 'may believe in me through their word'.

The church consists of people who will deliberately set themselves apart from all they know to be wrong, in order to be of service to their friends and acquaintances who are as yet strangers to Jesus. He himself did that for all of us. He expects to see that attitude mirrored in his followers (verse 19).

The church is meant to be united, in the same way that Jesus was united with his heavenly Father (verses 20 and 21). That unity does not mean uniformity, but it does mean identity of purpose, mutual love and recognisable belonging. Christian unity in this sense is not a secondary issue. It is absolutely vital. Jesus is insisting that nothing less than the love, trust, shared goals and mutual commitment of the church will convince people that God loves them and has sent Jesus for their rescue.

The church consists of people who model the love of God, the love which pours itself out on the undeserving (verse 26). That is meant to be the supreme mark of the followers of Jesus. That is how you are meant to be able to spot them.

The church consists of people in whom Jesus himself lives (verse 26). They are not copying him, strictly speaking. They are allowing his unseen presence, his 'Holy Spirit' to come and inhabit their very lives, and allow his fragrance to flow from them. God wants people to be able to look at the church, and immediately be made aware of and attracted to Jesus.

And finally, the church consists of people who will share the home of God for all eternity (verse 26). That is their destiny. Nothing less. You see, God will not scrap what is precious to him at the end of the day. And the 'little flock' of Jesus is supremely precious to him.

What an incredible vision of what the church ought to be and might be. And what an incredible anticlimax the church so often is! But Christians can take heart. Jesus has never revised his plan for his church. And he has never given up on it. As he predicted, the powers of hell will never prevail against it. They never have, and they never will. For although it is so often such a mess, it remains the divine society. If it were a merely human organisation it is such a shambles that it would have folded up centuries ago! But Christ brought it into being. Christ died to win the hearts of its members. Christ lives in them. Christ is at work purifying and guiding the church. So there is no reason for discouragement, let alone despair. It is a bit like the man who had a marker on his desk. One side of it read, 'God bless this mess.' The other read, 'God hasn't finished with me yet.'

6

The first Christian church

When we read something like Jesus' hopes for his church, outlined in the last chapter, it can all seem very idealistic – indeed impossible. Not so. It has happened. The early pages of the book of the Acts of the Apostles give us some fascinating glimpses of what it was like.

> They devoted themselves to the apostles' teaching and to the fellowship, to the breaking of bread and to prayer. Everyone was filled with awe, and many wonders and signs were done by the apostles. All the believers were together and had everything in common. Selling their possessions and goods, they gave to anyone as he had need. Every day they continued together in the temple courts. They broke bread in their homes and ate together with glad and sincere hearts, praising God and enjoying the favour of all the people. And the Lord added to their number daily those who were being saved. (Acts 2:42–7)

A little later on we find much the same picture: 'All the believers were one in heart and mind. No-one claimed that any of his possessions was his own, but they shared everything they had. With great power the apostles continued to testify to the resurrection of the Lord Jesus, and much grace was upon them all' (4:32–3).

Is it any wonder that people were attracted, and this new movement got off to such a magnificent start? Their warmth, their generosity, their care for the poor and needy, their complete break with materialism, their fervent prayer, their joyful praise of a God they seemed to know – why, it was unparalleled in the ancient world. And as for this power in testimony, this unshakable assurance that Jesus was risen from the dead – was alive and anyone could meet him – this was utterly revolutionary stuff. You could not remain neutral about it. You either denounced them as liars and traitors to their heritage, or else you joined them in this new and exciting movement.

We get a similar impression when we read about the first Christians who broke out of the Jewish chrysalis and started up on Gentile soil. It happened in Antioch, the third greatest city of the Roman Empire, and we read all about it in Acts 11. The account is too long to quote in full, but it tells the exciting story of how Christianity first came to this sophisticated Greek capital city. Here are some of the qualities that stand out. The first missionaries had to trust God for everything: they were homeless refugees from Jerusalem, where the rise of the new movement had led to persecution. They were unembarrassed to chat about 'the Lord Jesus' in the streets. 'Jesus' means 'God to the rescue'. 'Lord' means 'boss'. That was their message: of a God who loves human beings enough to come to their rescue in the person of Jesus of Nazareth, even if it involved death on a cross. This Jesus is Lord of the universe, and he has the right to be 'boss' in the lives of everyone. There was enormous response, and Barnabas and Saul spent eighteen months building up the new believers into a lively and well-informed church. They heard, through a travelling prophet, that a great famine was about to strike, which would affect Jerusalem particularly badly, since the first church members there had generously (if somewhat unwisely!) shared not only their income but their capital and property. So at once these Greek Christians in Antioch sent a substantial contribution to the distressed Jewish Christians in Jerusalem. How about that for unity, generosity and self-sacrifice? Remember they had been kicked out of Jerusalem in the first place! I find it astonishing that they should give so generously to the church there.

There are other lovely things about this early church in Antioch. Their fellowship was outstanding. For the first time in history Jews and Gentiles ate together, laughed and shared together in Antioch. Their leadership was impressive, too, and very unlike contemporary church leadership. It was no solitary vicar, but a team of five men who led that church, and they were of different colours, nationalities and social strata! The worship of the church was great. They really concentrated on the Lord, we are told: not on the flowers or the hat of the woman two rows in front! They prayed,

not just casually but with real sincerity, marked by fasting. They were genuinely open for God to intervene in the service and speak in the stillness as they waited on him. In this case, it was that they should be willing to give up two of their best leaders, Barnabas and Paul, and send them out on a missionary trip to destinations unknown. Unlike many churches today, they obeyed!

Do sit down and read the Acts of the Apostles. I think it is one of the most stirring books ever written. It gives enormous insight into the lifestyle and outreach of these first dynamic Christians. It shows that what Jesus envisaged for his church is possible. It has happened. And lest you think that was just a flash in the pan, just the initial enthusiasm which soon wore off, let me close this chapter with an account which comes to us from the second century, in the *Letter to Diognetus*.

The distinction between Christians and other men does not lie in country or language or customs ... They follow local customs in clothing, food, and in the rest of life; yet they exhibit the wonderful paradoxical nature of their own citizenship. They live in their own countries, but as if they were resident aliens. They share all things as citizens, and yet endure all things as if they were an underclass. Every foreign country is their homeland, and every homeland a foreign country. They marry like everyone else, and have children, but they do not abort their young. They keep a common table but not a common bed. They live in the world but not in a worldly way. They enjoy a full life on earth, but their citizenship is in heaven. They obey the appointed laws but they surpass the laws in their own lifestyle. They love everyone – and are universally derided. They are unknown – and roundly criticised. They are put to death – and gain life. They are poor but make many rich. They lack all things and yet have all things in abundance. They are dishonoured – and are glorified in their dishonour . . . They are abused and they call down blessings in return. When they do good they are beaten up as ne'er-do-wells: when they are beaten up they rejoice as men who are given a new life . . . In short, what the soul is in the body, that the Christians are in the world. The soul lives in the body but is not confined by the body, and the Christians live in the world but are not confined by the world . . . God has appointed them to this great calling, and it would be wrong for them to decline it.

I dare say that description may be a bit idealised. It may be eighteen hundred years old. But isn't it a marvellous glimpse of what the church has been? A hint, too of what it could be again, if we are prepared to pay the price?

7

God's counter-culture

Let's recap for a moment.

The church is not a building – the building is simply the place where the church meets. The church is not a clergyman or woman – they are simply the leaders of the church. The church is not an hour on a Sunday morning – though that may well be when they meet up.

No, the church is people. People who have come to put their faith in Jesus Christ, have welcomed his unseen Spirit into their lives, and have been baptised into a visible community. This community is worldwide. It embraces all colours and backgrounds and classes. All Christians are equally members of it.

Yes, the church is a worldwide family, committed to follow a leader who is 'out of this world'. His standards are out of this world. So is his goal. It is to bring the whole of society back under God's kingly rule. Back to the God from whom we have all declared independence.

The world rightly belongs to God who made it and brought each of us into being. The trouble is, we have all become rebels against him in our thoughts, words, actions and attitudes. But God loves us, and came to this world to rescue us from our predicament. This 'Operation Rescue' is often called 'salvation' in Christian circles. It means wholeness – bringing us back from the alienation and fragmentation of marred humanity into a new community, a new family, the church. The church is meant to show the reality and life-changing power of God. We cannot do this convincingly on our own. Part of the wonder of the church at its best is the complexity of people it embraces and welds into a task-force with a common aim and lifestyle. The lifestyle is determined by the standards laid down by Jesus. The aim is to draw other rebel members of God's kingly rule back to him.

And that is not something that can be accomplished by our Western individualism. That comes as a bit of a shock. We have had it dinned into us that we must stand on our own two feet, show our initiative and independence, and climb over other people who get in our way. But the gospel says 'no' to all that. It tells us we do not need to climb over other people in order to achieve. We can see other people not as our rivals but as our brothers and sisters. We can find our fulfilment not in personal supremacy but in the growth of God's kingdom. The gospel, to put it bluntly, is ruthlessly opposed to our prized individualism. We need each other.

You sometimes hear it said in Christian circles, 'The Lord has saved my soul.' But you never find that in the New Testament. God is not concerned with some internal magic called 'saving the soul'. He is concerned to 'save' people, whole people. He wants to change the direction of their lives from self to God and other people. And once you allow him to start that transformation in you, he puts you with other people in his church.

It makes sense, doesn't it? A single strand of cotton is easily broken. But a thousand strands of cotton make a strong rope. So it is with God's church. He is out to form a counter-culture, a body of men, women and children who will dance to a different tune, the music of the kingdom of God. They will march to a different drum, the call of Jesus Christ. They will bond together to do it. And if that brings them into conflict with the selfishness and hedonism of society that leaves God out, so be it. We cannot begin to make any impact on secular society by ourselves, but together we can. That is part, at least, of what the church is for.

8

Signing on

Several times thus far I have referred to becoming a Christian, or a member of the church. It is high time to clarify what we mean by this, because there is a lot of confusion around.

If you ask someone in the Catholic tradition – Roman Catholic, Orthodox or Anglo Catholic – they are likely to give you a short and simple answer. You become a Christian, a member of the church, an inheritor of the kingdom of God (and all those other marvellous phrases) when you get baptised. In other words, it is something done for you by the church or its representatives. They immerse you, or sprinkle you with water, in the name of the Father and the Son and the Holy Spirit, and, hey-presto, you are henceforward a Christian.

Now that has got something to be said for it. It is decisive. You are either 'in' or 'out'. No middle ground. What is more, it is a healthy reminder that we do not make ourselves Christians, members of the family of God. It is something we have to receive as a gift from the hand of God himself. But it has one terrible weakness. It suggests you can become a Christian without wanting to, intending to, or even, if you are baptised as an infant, being able to influence the thing in any way. Clearly that will not do. It is very obvious that there are millions of people who have been baptised but who have no Christian faith and show no sign of Christian behaviour.

If you ask almost any of the Protestant denominations, you will get a very different answer to the question of what makes you a Christian. They are not likely to talk a lot about baptism. They are all too well aware of the problem of baptised unbelievers. No, they will tell you that conversion or regeneration is needed. 'Conversion' means your turning away from sin and self-centredness and turning in faith and gratitude to Christ who has died for you and lives to be your companion throughout this life and the next. And 'regeneration' is the technical name Christians use for the new life that God gives you when you turn to him in this way. Conversion is our side. Regeneration, or the new birth, is God's side. But that view has weaknesses, too. What about those too young or too old or too mentally incapable to go through this repenting business? Are they excluded? And where does baptism fit in?

But if you ask a Pentecostal how you become a Christian, you will find a still different emphasis. Pentecostals do not major on baptism or on repentance and faith, thought they mention both. But they will insist that the really important thing is to receive the divine gift, the Holy Spirit. If you have not got him in your life, you can be baptised and recite all the creeds until the cows come home, but it does not make you a Christian. This view is saying something important. But it, too, has weaknesses. How are you going to identify the church across the world? How will you know if people have received this Holy Spirit? Do they not need to be bonded in some sort of organisation?

All three views – Catholic, Protestant, and Pentecostal – are inadequate if you take them on their own. But if you hold them together, they make a marvellously clear definition of what it is to be a Christian. You are a Christian if you have come in repentance for sin and trust in Christ to the living God, who accepts you, puts his Spirit into your heart, and expects you to be baptised into the visible community of his church. Full Christian initiation involves conversion, reception of the Holy Spirit and baptism. They may come in different orders. But they belong together, as three critical strands in Christian initiation: the churchly strand, baptism; the personal strand, repentance and faith; and the divine strand, the Holy Spirit. That is what it means to become a Christian.

Have you, perhaps, had a sudden overwhelming experience of God and know that you are different, know that something has happened in your heart? Right, then you need consciously to turn from whatever you know to be wrong, and deliberately entrust your life to this Christ whom you have begun to experience. You also need to be baptised into the congregation of God's people.

Were you, perhaps, baptised in infancy, brought by believing parents who trusted that you would one day come to full Christian commitment? Right, you need to turn to Christ, confess your sins, rejoice in what he has done on the cross to make you clean before God, and ask him to put his Spirit into your life so that you can begin to live as one of his followers. You do not need the baptism bit all over again. You have got that already!

Have you, perhaps, turned to God in the past and been baptised, then or earlier? What you need is to make sure that you have invited God's Holy Spirit into your life, for we have the apostle Paul's word for it that 'if anyone does not have the Spirit of Christ, he does not belong to Christ' (Romans 8:9).

So where do you stand personally? Of course you will find the church dreary and unfulfilling if you have not taken those three steps of Christian initiation.

You may believe in God and the story of Jesus. You may believe he died for the sins of the world, and that he rose from the dead. But could this all be a formality to you? You have never reached the point of admitting that your own sins and failures were part of the terrible load of the world's evil that took the Son of God to Calvary. You have never told him how ashamed and sorry you are. And you may never have understood that because he carried that load of your guilt you will never have to do so. You can be forgiven, accepted in Christ, even though you feel unacceptable in yourself. And perhaps you have come to see that Jesus not only rose from the dead long ago, but he is still alive. You see him shining in the lives of some of your friends. You can see he has made such a difference to them.

Right, what is needed? God has no favourites. If he has done it for them he will do it for you. But you need to come and ask him. Ask him to forgive your sins. Ask him to accept you and bring you into the Christian family. And ask him to fill you as full as you are able to receive with his Holy Spirit. And then, if you have not been baptised, it is high time to seal the transaction with the glorious public rite of baptism. If you have already been baptised, you do not need it. You already had one strand of Christian initiation. You needed the other two, of conversion and the Holy Spirit.

But maybe you are already a believer, but you are dry. You do not experience the joy you feel you should have. You find prayer a big struggle, the Bible unattractive, Christian service a chore. Perhaps you need to ask the Lord to fill you with his Holy Spirit in every aspect of your being? Could that be what is lacking in your full Christian initiation?

Or maybe you came to Christian things in a context that was casual about baptism. What you need, surely, is to be baptised, in obedience to your Lord's command (Matthew 28:19). Most people who come to this sacrament as adults find tremendous joy in it as a physical mark of belonging to Christ and his church. It is a bit like an adoption certificate for a child or a wedding ring for a bride. It shows you that you belong. And it shows other people as well.

Baptism, repentance and faith, and reception of the

Holy Spirit – these are the three strands in Christian initiation. The important thing is not just to recognise this and to agree – but to *sign on for yourself*. Until that happens you will be missing out on true Christianity, and you will always find yourself assessing it from the outside.

Some years ago I walked around King's College Chapel in Cambridge. I had heard of the fabulous glass, but all I could see was windows that looked black and dull. It was only when I went inside that I could appreciate the wonder of that glass. It is only when you enter into the promised salvation of God that you will discover its joy and power. Sign on! It is very simple. He is only a prayer away. Tell him you are sorry. Tell him how thankful you are for what he did at Calvary. Turn to him as the living one, the Easter Jesus, and ask him to place the Holy Spirit in your heart, and be assured that he will never turn a deaf ear to such a prayer, for 'everyone who calls on the name of the Lord shall be saved' (Romans 10:13). And then, if you have not been baptised, get on with it!

9

Body life

The New Testament has many pictures of what it means to be a Christian, and the fascinating thing is that they are all corporate ones. None of this stuff about 'I can be a Christian in my back garden: I don't need to go to church' or 'My religion is my own affair'. No. Once you sign on with Jesus Christ you find you are a soldier in his army, a stone in his building, a member of his household, a child in his family, a branch in his tree and a whole host of evocative metaphors like that.

But the most fascinating one of all is the idea of the church as Christ's body. It was a particularly favourite image of St Paul's, and he develops it at length when writing to Christians at Corinth. They were argumentative and arrogant. They felt they could do without one another. They flaunted their spiritual gifts without thinking of the effect on other people. Pride and jealousy flourished among them. So did division. They took up party labels to show how different they were from other believers – and how superior! It was not a good situation. Indeed it was a disgrace to the Christian cause. So Paul writes to take them to task. He tells them they are Christ's body. Think of it for a moment. It is a brilliant illustration, and has many applications.

It is only through my body that you can grasp what the inner, unseen Michael Green is really like. It is the same in the Christian body, the church. It is only through the church they *can* see that people can understand what the Jesus they *can't* see is like.

The idea of the body speaks of interdependence and harmony. In my physical body, no limb has all the qualities needed. But none is readily dispensable. It is the same in the Christian body.

The idea of the body means that there is no room either for pride on the one hand or jealousy on the other. The arm is not proud because it is stronger than the toe, or the fingernail jealous of the eye. They all have their part to play in a properly functioning body. It is the same in the Christian body. There is no room for pride among the gifted or jealousy among the humbler members of the community. We need each other if the body is to flourish.

The idea of the body means that ministry or service is not the privilege of the few, but the responsibility of every organ in the body. Just as every part of my physical body has its own job to do, so it should be in the Christian body. There is no room either for prima donnas on the stage or drones in the hive. You cannot be a Christian without having a ministry to exercise for the Lord.

The idea of the body suggests mutual respect between

the members: the whole thing operates on the principle of variety in unity. How inept the body would be if every limb had the same job. How devastated it would be if two-thirds of the limbs did nothing! That has a powerful message for the church, where so often it is the faithful few who do everything – and sometimes like to keep it that way for the sake of power and influence.

The body owes its life and direction to the brain which governs every movement and shows itself in every gesture. St Paul, in his letters to the Christians at Ephesus and Colossae, develops this image of the body, to stress the leadership function of the head, Jesus Christ. We cannot see him, any more than you can see my brain: but everything I do shows the activity and control of the brain. That's what the church is meant to be like.

In the body, every part is connected to the brain directly through the nervous system. It should be the same in the body of Christ, the church. Each of us is meant to be in direct touch with Christ.

Finally, the body is not static. It grows in harmony, size and usefulness. It should be like that with Christ's body, the church, 'when every part is working properly' as St Paul cautions (Ephesians 4:16).

Isn't that a marvellous picture? No wonder Paul was so fond of it. He uses it in his letters to the Romans, the Corinthians, the Colossians and the Ephesians. Once you start thinking of the church as the body of Christ, and of Jesus as its unseen but controlling head, you at once have a yardstick by which to judge contemporary

church life. The trouble is that in so many churches every part is not working properly. There are plenty of maladies in the body of Christ.

One of them is *amputation* from the body. Folk cut themselves off from really committing themselves to one another. They are occasional visitors, not core members. That is a real shame. Both the amputated limb and the remaining trunk miss out.

Another is *elephantiasis* in the body. One member, often the minister, grows to an excessive size. They throw their weight around and call the shots in the church meeting. That is a great pity too. The result is that other parts of the body don't get the chance to make their own contribution. So the people who love to be top dog find themselves doing all sorts of things for which they are not fitted, while those with the requisite gifts do not get the chance to use them.

Atrophy is a very common disease in the body. Many members just sit there in services and think that is all there is to the Christian life. There is no exercise, no muscle-building activity from people like that. As a result, even the strength they have wastes away. Like a person who has been in bed inactive for a month, they can hardly stand if they try to get up – let alone do anything useful.

Fractures all too often occur in the body. Members fall out with one another and they blandly assume that nobody is harmed but themselves. This is far from the truth. Think of what agony your whole body is in if you have got one fractured toe. What must the living head,

Jesus Christ, feel about his body, plagued by multiple fractures?

Arthritis is another ailment all too common in our human bodies, especially as we get older. And it is found in long-standing Christian bodies as frequently as it is in brand-new assemblies. Perhaps more so. It is an abrasiveness, a grinding of bone upon bone. And it hurts. Of course, in a well-regulated, healthy body this does not happen. Bone does not grate upon bone, but upon a seating of gristle instead. The name of that gristle in the body of Christ is love. 'Speaking the truth in love, we will in all things grow up into him who is the Head, that is, Christ. From him the whole body, joined and held together by every supporting ligament, grows and builds itself up in love, as each part does its work' (Ephesians 4:15–16).

This image of the church as Christ's body on earth is immensely attractive. If any church is to be a true expression of the life of the risen Jesus Christ, it must take the lessons of the body very seriously indeed, and take great pains to avoid the diseases which are as destructive in the Christian body as they are in our human body.

10

The family meal

I remember how shocked I was to discover in some survey or other that in many homes nowadays the family simply never had a meal together. They were in and out, doing their own thing, eating junk food, caught up in the frenetic pace of modern life. Your family can't have much in the way of togetherness, shared experience and mutual enrichment if you never meet over a meal. The meal is the supreme mark of belonging, in the East, and even in our fragmented Western society to have a meal together is one of the joys of life and a means of deepening relationships. Think of Sunday lunch!

The church, too, has its family meal. It originated with Jesus himself, and he told his followers to do it in remembrance of him. Very early on it seems to have become a weekly time of celebration for the Christians. They would gather after work, have an evening together in a home, share news over the meal, encourage one another, pull out of the church box a letter from one of the apostles, like St Paul, and read it to those present. The evening would end with sharing in a common loaf and drinking from a common cup to recall Jesus' presence.

It all goes back, of course, to the Last Supper. It was not only the night of Jesus' arrest: it was Passover time. And Passover was an age-old festival of the Jews to celebrate their national deliverance from Egypt under the Pharaohs where they were subjected to slavery and often to death. On one terrible night just before they broke out in what we have come to call the Exodus, they obeyed God's instructions to paste the blood of a lamb on the doorposts of their houses, so as to turn away God's destroying angel as he slew the first-born children of Egypt. A terrible night they never forgot. So Passover was special. It was really the feast that constituted them a separate people. It was freedom night, as they escaped from the bondage and death of Egypt – through the blood of a lamb, painted on the doors of their homes.

The Lord told them to keep this as a permanent reminder of his deliverance. They have done so ever since. Each year they had a Passover feast, with a lamb to eat, reminding them of the lamb sacrificed for their deliverance long ago, when God's judgment 'passed over' every house that was painted with the blood. The meal was garnished with bitter herbs, reminding them of the bitter experiences they had in Egypt. There was unleavened bread and wine, as well, in these Passover meals. And there was the story, told on each occasion, of the great act of rescue which God had long ago done for their nation. You could have a Passover meal either as a family or if a dozen Jewish friends were together. And the recollection was so vital that the president said, 'This the Almighty did for *me* when *I* went out of Egypt.' The rescue of long ago is all personalised and brought into present application.

Such was the background to the Last Supper. Imagine, then, the awed amazement of his friends when, instead of saying the traditional words, 'This is the bread of affliction which our fathers ate in the wilderness', Jesus took the unleavened bread, broke it and said, 'This is my body, which is given for you.' By replacing the traditional formula with his never-to-be-forgotten words, Jesus meant them to see his death as the fulfilment of the great deliverance which the death of the Passover lambs had anticipated. His death would secure a rescue for his followers from a worse bondage and a worse fate than there had ever been in Egypt; it would mean release from the guilt and power of evil in their lives. This was the true liberation, to which the Old Testament had pointed forward. And the very next day it all began to come true. Jesus is constantly seen by the New Testament writers as the Passover Lamb who fulfilled all the Old Testament predictions.

We do not know when the yearly Passover feast of the Jews became the weekly celebration of the Christians, but it certainly happened within a few years of Jesus' death and resurrection. Perhaps the resurrection was the key to it. After all, his resurrection led to the change of rest day from the Jewish Saturday to the Christian Sunday. How fitting to celebrate the Lord's great meal when they met together on the Lord's great day.

And if we want to understand the meaning of the Communion service, as most Christians have come to call it, we need look no further than the old Jewish Passover meal which it replaces. First, like the Passover, the Communion looks back to a sacrifice, the sacrifice of Christ on the cross. It was there that he made possible our release. It was there that he won the great battle over the enemy. It was there that he dealt with human guilt by taking personal responsibility for it. The Communion is not itself a sacrifice, any more than successive Passovers were: but both of them vividly recall the unique sacrifice which brought them into being. So we should come to each Communion service with a real sense of the wrong things we have done and what it cost the Lord to set us free from them. There should be a deep sense of gratitude to the Saviour for his profound love for us which led him to that awesome sacrifice of Calvary.

Second, like the Passover, the Communion is a meal to strengthen us for the journey. The Jews were bidden to eat the complete lamb to strengthen them for the crossing of the Red Sea that was to come. Read all about it in Exodus 12. In a similar way, Christians have always seen the Communion as food for our spiritual lives. Just as our physical bodies are strengthened by our meals, so our spiritual lives are fed by the bread and wine which symbolise and make available to us none other than Jesus himself. That is the deep mystery of this wonderful meal. He feeds us with himself so that we can go out and represent him in society. It is, as Jesus put it, 'my body . . . my blood' that we receive at every Communion, and by it we are strengthened for our human pilgrimage.

Third, there was always a forward look to the Passover meal. The old rabbis had a saying, 'On this night they were saved and on this night they shall be saved.' The Passover was a pointer to the feast of salvation in the future, just as surely as it was a memorial of God's deliverance in the past. So strongly was this emphasised that each Jewish family would leave an empty chair at the Passover meal, in case Elijah, the great prophet of the last days, should return! And this same forward look is characteristic of the Communion. As St Paul put it 'We proclaim the Lord's death until he comes' (1 Corinthians 11:26). Just as the Passover was the guarantee of the Messiah's coming, so the Communion is the pledge of his return at the end of all history. That is why the old Aramaic word *Maranatha* was used at the Communion in the ancient church. It means 'O Lord, come!' At every Communion Christians turn their eyes to heaven, to the final feast with their beloved Lord and his people for ever.

What a wonderful family meal this is! Rescue from our accusing past, strength for the daily round, and a foretaste of heaven. No wonder the Christian family loves to celebrate it often. It embodies the very heart of our faith.

11

Faith in action

It was after church one Sunday night. The man had got into his car, and when he saw me walking towards him, he wound down the window and said, 'That's that for the week. I don't want to have anything to do with Christianity until next Sunday night!' He is not the only one who thinks like that. There is a widespread impression that churchgoing makes absolutely no difference to the way you live. It simply means you give up an hour or so on a Sunday to sing hymns, listen to prayers and engage with a sermon – and, of course, you pay for the privilege as well! Nothing could be further from the Christianity we find in the New Testament.

For one thing, as we have seen, church is not something you *go to* but something you *are*. It is a body in which you are a limb. Naturally, therefore, it must make a difference – if you really are a limb. The trouble is that there are still people in church on a Sunday who are not part of the body at all, because they have never allowed the Spirit of the risen Christ to have access to their lives. They are like wooden legs or glass eyes. They look as if they belong to the body but they do not have its life coursing through them.

And that leads us on to the second reason why there is bound to be a difference if you are a Christian. You see, you are a disciple, a follower of Jesus Christ. Inevitably, therefore, you try to allow your life to be modelled on his. Of course you can't hope to succeed on your own. That is why Christ puts his Holy Spirit into the lives of his followers, so that they can begin to reproduce something of his quality of life. They are still very weak and fallible human beings, and so the image is always going to be blurred, but the seed of his life is within them and gradually it begins to show. That is why the New Testament talks about the fruit which the Holy Spirit produces in our lives. 'The fruit of the Spirit is love, joy, peace, patience, kindness, goodness, faithfulness, gentleness and self-control.' The first Christians were very insistent that unless there is some real change in our lives after entrusting them to Jesus Christ, our profession of faith is worthless.

What good is it, my brothers, if a man claims to have faith but has no deeds? Can such a faith save him? Suppose a brother or sister is without clothes and daily food. If one of you says to him, 'Go, I wish you well; keep warm and well fed,' but does nothing about his physical needs, what good is it? In the same way, faith by itself, if it is not accompanied by action, is dead.

So writes the very practically minded James in his letter

(2:14–17). John writes in a similar vein:

This is how we know what love is: Jesus Christ laid down his life for us. And we ought to lay down our lives for our brothers. If anyone has material possessions and sees his brother in need but has no pity on him, how can the love of God be in him? Dear children, let us not love with words or tongue but with actions and in truth. (1 John 3:16–18)

Yes, real Christianity makes a difference. It makes a difference to the way we treat human need, and it makes a difference to the way we live our personal lives. Listen to St Paul on the subject. 'You must rid yourselves of all such things as these: anger, rage, malice, slander and filthy language from your lips. Do not lie to each other, since you have taken off your old self with its practices and have put on the new self, which is being renewed in knowledge in the image of its Creator.' The old lifestyle has to go, and is progressively replaced by the new Christlike way of living. Paul continues,

Therefore, as God's chosen people, holy and dearly beloved, clothe yourselves with compassion, kindness, humility, gentleness and patience. Bear with each other and forgive whatever grievances you may have against one another. Forgive as the Lord forgave you. And over all these virtues put on love, which binds them all together in perfect unity.

He concludes, 'And whatever you do, whether in word or deed, do it all in the name of the Lord Jesus, giving thanks to God the Father through him.' You'll find all that in Colossians 3, but the same themes occur in almost all the New Testament letters. Indeed, Paul once uses that very image and addresses his readers as 'living letters': people can look at them and read something of the message of Jesus.

That is why, despite so many failures in the Christian camp, you always find the true followers of Jesus trying to put their faith into action. I suppose Mother Teresa is the most world-famous example of this, but there are many millions, known and unknown, whose lives radiate Christ's love and practical goodness. Think of someone like Martin Luther King, who became a Christian martyr in the cause of racial equality. Think of Dietrich Bonhoeffer who also made the supreme sacrifice against Nazi tyranny. Think of someone like Sally Trench, author of *Bury Me in My Boots*, who gave up a privileged background to live and work for Christ among the homeless, and has recently gone to do the same in Bosnia in the aftermath of war. The fight against racism is often led by Christians – think of Desmond Tutu who also, in characteristic Christian role, chaired the South African Reconciliation Commission which has done so much to restore relationships in that divided land. It was church people who were so moved by the plight of the starving in Sudan and the orphanages in Romania that they took a radical lead in transforming those situations. It was primarily the church people who have made such a powerful plea for Jubilee 2000, the remission of Third World debt. And in the midst of the sexual anarchy of our times, it is the Christians who have founded True Love Waits, pledged to sexual purity before marriage. It is Christians like Baroness Cox and her Christian Solidarity Worldwide who seek to alert the world to the massive persecution going on in more than seventy countries of the world, when most people would rather turn a blind eye to it all. In the inner city it is the Christians who you will find staying on, struggling on against the odds, when so many others move out. It is Christian organisations like Tear Fund, Oxfam, Cafod and World Vision that have taken immense initiatives in meeting all types of human deprivation in the less fortunate parts of the world. After the war in Kosovo more than seventy Christian churches worked together in Albania to bring food and some measure of relief to the overwhelming hordes of refugees. In the hard, untamed parts of the world where comfortable people do not want to work, you will find Christian doctors and nurses manning bush hospitals and working impossible hours in intolerable conditions. They do it because they love the Lord, and they want their lives to mediate that love by meeting human need. They have Christ's new life in them. They are seeking to follow his lifestyle.

We are not all able, or even willing, to go to the ends of the earth for the gospel, but it is incumbent on all who profess the name of Christ to be committed to personal transformation and practical goodness. My wife has just done a shop at Sainsbury's for a couple who are overwhelmed by the birth of twins, and taken them a meal and a chocolate cake. Nothing unusual about that, you may say. True. However, it is a small but real outworking of faith in action. And that is what church people are called to do.

12

The church in the home

There are lots of ways of being church. We have got used to the idea of church being an hour or so a week where the speaking parts are restricted to the minister and a choir, and the rest of us turn up and participate as best we can. But that is certainly not the only way for a church to operate. Arguably it is not the best way.

The ancient Jews had a brilliant insight. They realised that you need a regular time for competent teaching and worship. That is what happened in the synagogue on a Saturday. They realised that you needed occasionally to have a great celebration with a festival crowd all together in one place, to remind people what a great organisation they belonged to. That is what the feasts like Tabernacles, Passover and Pentecost were intended to do. But they also majored on the small group meeting in the home on a Friday evening. It might be a family group or a group of friends. There was food, a chance for relaxation, chat, worship and quiet reflection.

The Christian church has been reasonably good at developing one of those models – the synagogue meeting – into our regular church services. But we have

not been much good at the other two. The sense of riotous celebration is rare in Christian circles. It is not often that you find thousands of believers coming together to rejoice in their common heritage. And you do not often find churches breaking down into small home groups. That is a great pity, because the home group is invaluable.

Most great movements in human history are based on the small cell of like-minded people, bound together for a common cause. That is certainly true of communism, which captured a third of the world in our lifetime. It is very much the case with the massive growth of Pentecostal Christians in Latin America, where belonging to a small group, meeting informally in the home, is immensely important to all the members. You find exactly the same in the fast-growing churches in the Far East, places like Singapore and Sabah, and all over China. Small is beautiful. You can't love a hundred and fifty people whom you meet occasionally in a cold and strange building. But you can love a dozen people who meet regularly and informally in your home.

Think of the advantages of the informal home meeting. For one thing you do not need a minister to lead it. People can take the lead in turn, and thus develop their skills and competence. Nobody preaches at you from six feet above contradiction. You wrestle together over issues, perhaps in ethics, perhaps in the Bible, perhaps in contemporary life. Nobody is left out in the cold. Nobody is pew fodder. Everyone matters. You can get to know everyone, remember their birthday, take them a meal when they are sick. Members get to understand what Christian fellowship is about – a real sharing in Christ and in each other's lives. Loneliness is banished. Gifts emerge of which their owners were previously unaware. The group begins to see needs in the church or in the community at large that it can fill. The companionship is not only experienced over a meal or at a Bible study, but at the theatre, in painting someone's house, or on holiday together. To be sure, prayer will be part of it. So will Bible reading. But a group can easily be killed if these are the main objectives. Have you not met the person who prays all the way round the world and whose Elizabethan English is so perfect that nobody dares follow them? Have you not been at the Bible study which has been totally dominated by some know-all, and ruined for everyone else? Certainly there needs to be worship. After all we meet as members of Christ's body. That is why St Paul encourages each of the members of the group to come together with a contribution – 'a hymn, a word of instruction, a revelation, a tongue or an interpretation', all of which are designed to strengthen the church (1 Corinthians 14:26). But the worship is only part of it. We need to share our *lives*. There needs to be recreation – and that is where a good meal comes in. There needs to be good discussion and the opportunity to make suggestions and float bright ideas. There needs to be freedom for someone to come in from a hard day's work, flop down and say 'I'm fed up' – and find that the group drop their plans for the evening in order to minister to him or her. Once you get that sort of thing happening in a group a very intimate bond develops. People share with the group things they hardly dare mention to their spouses. It is an enormous support. And all the members are built up.

I recall trudging miles over the north Yorkshire moors with a good friend. He took me to a gaunt farmhouse standing miles away from anywhere: there were no other signs of habitation in sight. But when we got inside we found a dozen people crammed in, obviously revelling in each other's company and the bit of Scripture they were studying.

I think of a gardener's hut in Chile, with a rat running across the floor and a child hiding behind the curtain. About ten people were crammed into that little hut, including a visiting bishop and clergyman. But it was entirely lay-led. There was no question of the ordained men taking over. They all shared their lives and experience together, and we were privileged to be part of it.

I think of a place in Sabah, which used to be British North Borneo. I was staying with a gifted young pastor, an Anglican as it happened. He had more than two hundred house 'churches' in the Christian community for which he was responsible. They had a great bonding with one another, and did almost all the things one associates with the church in their homes when they met. The job of the pastor was to train the leaders – and then to leave them to get on with it. No wonder such groups grow apace.

And if you think that this is overseas and it does not

happen in Britain, you are wrong. Many of our churches see the home groups into which their congregations are subdivided as essential for mutual pastoring and growth. They are only too willing to be active on some project for the larger church. They are hospitable to non-churchgoing friends, and because it is not a formal service led by a minister in a church building, people feel free to come. That is how the numbers grow. And of course such a group is a marvellous way of building up members of the congregation, as they learn together and offer their talents: perhaps of singing, DIY, leading a discussion, secretarial skills, cooking, or the prophetic insight that comes to some people in pictorial form. Yes, I know that sort of thing happens in Britain. It did in the church which I had the privilege of leading. I think we had some forty such groups. They dealt with a lot of the simpler pastoral problems that arise in any church, and they enabled lay people to grow and discover their ministry in the body of Christ.

If I had to choose between the relaxed church in the home and the formal worship in the church building, I know which I would go for. Mercifully we do not have to choose. They complement each other.

13

Church leadership

Christian leaders frequently get a bad press. If you go by what you read in the newspapers, many of them are corrupt. If you go by what you see on the box, the vicar is a figure of fun, universally derided. Many people would agree that the clergy are 'six days invisible, one day incomprehensible'. No wonder ministers are ill paid. They do not do a serious job.

That is of course ridiculous. Many clergy live blameless lives, are deeply sincere, and work extremely hard; some literally wear themselves out for the sake of their congregations. But what is the minister supposed to be? What is the actual job?

Well, look around you at the ministers you know. What do you see? Some are taken up with services and ritual. Some regard preaching as the main purpose of their existence. Some seem constantly to be on committees. Some favour further degrees. Some see their role as exclusively pastoral among their congregations. A few have evangelistic fervour. What is this enigmatic job?

There is a fascinating passage in St Paul's letter to the

Christians at Ephesus which has a good deal of light to shed on the subject. Christ 'gave some to be apostles, some to be prophets, some to be evangelists, and some to be pastors and teachers, to prepare God's people for works of service, so that the body of Christ may be built up' (Ephesians 4:11–12). Let's examine that little passage in some detail.

The first thing I see here is that Christian leadership is a *gift* from Christ. It is not something anyone has a right to. It is not something we can earn. It is one of Christ's gifts to his church. If we get clear about that we shall avoid two contrasting mistakes. In some denominations the pastor is hired and fired by the people: he is under them. In other denominations the priest dominates the people and makes all the decisions: he is over them. But this passage of Scripture insists that we must neither despise nor overvalue the Christian leader. We must see them as Christ's gift.

The second thing that stands out in this passage is that Christian leadership should be *shared*. Each of the categories – evangelists, pastors, teachers and so on – is in the plural. Indeed, the word from which our English 'priest' is derived, *presbyteros*, is always in the plural in the New Testament, when it refers to Christian leaders. The early church knew nothing of one-person leadership. It was always a team affair. So you find that the leadership at Antioch, mentioned in Acts 13:1, contains no less than five people. How wise that is. It means the congregation is spared domination by one person. It means that the group make up for the inadequacies of any one individual. It means that different aspects of character and leadership are available for the church: one person may be great on strategy, another on youth work, another on music, and so on. And it means that the mutual relationships of the team, if they are working well, can be a model at the heart of the congregation of how those home groups we were thinking about in the last chapter should operate. There is a lot to be said for shared leadership, though I do not pretend it is easy. You do not find it very often today. Instead you either find the dominating leader or the faceless committee. I have spent many years working in shared leadership situations and I believe they are extremely healthy for the church.

Another feature that emerges from those verses in Ephesians is this. The first Christians expected leadership to be *varied*. Today we have in almost all denominations a uniform training leading to a uniform type of leadership – by one person who is duly ordained. There is very little about ordination in the New Testament but the variety in the ministry of leadership is there for all to see. Some were called by Jesus himself as foundational leaders, the apostles. Some had the gift of insight and spoke from God into particular situations: they were the prophets. Some had a particular ability to bring people to decision about Jesus: they were the evangelists. Some had teaching skills: naturally they were the teachers. And some had the ability to draw alongside people and help them to grow and to resolve outstanding problems in their lives: those were the pastors. It is obvious that we need those varied ministries in our churches today. Happy the church that has a leadership team which is committed to the apostolic message which we have in our New Testaments, and comprises people with prophetic, pastoral, teaching and evangelistic gifts. They do not all have to be ordained, of course. They certainly do not all have to be paid. But they do need to be operational!

But what are these varied leadership gifts intended for? Ego trips for those who have them? An opportunity to display their gifts? Of course not. Taking services? There is, curiously enough, no hint of that in the New Testament. No, our passage in Ephesians makes it abundantly plain why Christ has given his church these varied ministries of leadership. It is *to equip God's people* for their works of service. That is it. Christian leaders exist as ordinary members of the body of Christ just like everyone else. They have no special status. But their particular function, as limbs in that body, is to equip other members to function properly as Christians in their home and professional lives, and so build up the church community in unity, love and knowledge. That is a noble task. Not many leaders embrace it. But the New Testament insists that the function of Christian leadership is to equip the Christians in their care to grow together in spiritual maturity and to show Christ's love and active goodness in society. That is what leaders are for.

14

Institution and life

There is all the world of difference between the church as an institution and the church as a bundle of spiritual life. So often the church is seen just an institution, with its rules and regulations, its financiers, its officers, its dress code, its legal status and all the rest. Our generation has made a fairly decisive break with all that. We are not into institutions these days, particularly authoritative ones, of which the church is a prime example. We want life.

Well, real Christianity is all about life. Jesus once said, 'I have come so that you may have life, and have it to the full.' But you might be pardoned if that aspect of the church had never struck you! Sadly, I have to admit that much church life is as dead as a doornail. I would not be writing as I am unless I cared passionately about the situation. Many churches themselves seem to be dead. They have few members. Hardly any men. No teenagers at all. No young families. No signs of joy and celebration. No congregational involvement in the activities of the church: everything is run from the front. No expectant prayer or joyful praise. No change in the pattern of activity from year to year. No impact on the surrounding community. No sense, even, of close companionship among the faithful few who attend. Alas, there are too many churches like that.

But that is not the best God has on offer. The New Testament tells us that Jesus offered us sparkling water that would never go stale, the very bread of life, joy that nobody can take from us, a priceless pearl, treasure hidden in a field, which we may stumble across. He speaks of a great party which God throws and then invites all and sundry to come and take part. That is what real Christianity is like. No wonder Jesus said, 'I have come that you may have life, and have it to the full.' The heart of Christianity, Jesus exclaimed in his famous prayer recorded in John 17, is that 'they may know you, the only true God, and Jesus Christ whom you have sent'. The trouble is that some churches seem not to know that life. At any rate, they do not introduce people to it. As a result they simply go through the motions: members may be regular in church attendance but devoid of a living personal relationship with Christ. And the church as institution seems, unfortunately, to be happy to go along with that state of affairs. It represents official religion. It is there to conduct baptisms, weddings and funerals. To be available for special occasions. To bless flags and to have quiet, early morning Communion services.

Now I do not want to knock churches like that. The people in control may want to achieve no more than that. There may be opposition among church members to anything more lively or relevant. The minister may have got discouraged, and be counting the months to retirement. It is surely better to have churches like that than no churches at all. They keep the rumour of God alive in the community. They can minister to people at critical moments of their lives, such as birth, marriage and death. I never like to write off a church like that, and call it dead. Maybe it is dead. But maybe, like an oak tree in winter, it is currently in a state of suspended animation, and when the spring comes it will revive. Anyhow, I believe in the God of resurrection. However dead a church may be, the Jesus who is Resurrection and Life can utterly transform the situation. Time and time again I have known that happen to churches in my own experience. I am delighted, but I am not surprised. After all, Christians serve the God who says, 'I am making everything new.'

But we may be sure of this. God does not intend his people to languish in a situation like this. He has made it perfectly plain in the Scriptures that a healthy church is one with shared leadership, vibrant prayer life, warm fellowship, practical service in the community, appropriate ministries for all ages, and a heart always reaching out to people who are not yet followers of Jesus.

A recent study of growing churches in the Durham area of Britain by Robert Warren came up with a common pattern that is repeated in many parts of the world. Whatever the denomination and whatever the style of worship, these seven characteristics manifested themselves in churches that were alive and growing.

- There was an *enabling* style of leadership.
- There was plenty of *lay participation*.
- There was openness to *change*.
- There was reliance on *small groups*.
- There was an *outward-looking* ethos.
- There was a *clear vision*, and shared sense of *direction*.
- There was a *quality* about all they did, notably in the conduct of Sunday worship.

The Durham material goes further. It draws attention to the fundamental cause of growth, underlying the characteristics mentioned above. Why is it that one church is dynamic and alive while another appears dead? The answer lies in the reality or otherwise of the church's encounter with the living God. Often, though by no means always, this starts with the minister. And it is this encounter with God which motivates those seven characteristics outlined above. It motivates:

- ministers to adopt an *enabling* style of leadership, confident that they have something to give away;
- lay people to have something in which to *participate*, namely their awareness of the reality of God;
- congregations to be willing to face the need for, and willingness to pay the price of, *change*;
- churches to be *outward-looking*, because they have been touched by God's compassion for his world and feel called into mission;
- church leadership teams to discover a sense of God's *direction* for the church;

- everyone to be committed to doing a *quality job*, making *sacrifices* but also experiencing the *satisfaction* of a job well done, which then gives motivation for further advance.

If you are looking for a 'church for amateurs', that is the sort of church you would be wise to join. It is not just an institution. It is life.

15

Church and kingdom

I do not want to end this short book without having a brief look at the relation between the church and the kingdom of God. The prophets of the Old Testament longed for the day when the unpredictable rule of the kings and the frequent disobedience of the people would undergo radical change. They looked for the day when God himself would be the wise and gracious ruler of his people, and they would be his loving and obedient servants.

That hope deepened during the troublesome times when Jesus was growing up. The little land of Palestine was restive under Roman rule, and men and women were hungry for the day when the prophetic hopes would be fulfilled. In a word they were looking for the kingdom of God, the day when God would unleash his kingly power and reign.

When Jesus started his ministry, his preaching was all about the kingdom of God. It was a big surprise to his hearers, for it subverted all their ideas of kingship. They thought God's king would beat up the Romans. Jesus taught them that he was coming to deal radically with

wickedness, and this was to be found as much in the Jews as in the Romans. They thought God's ruler would throw his weight about and get people to serve him. He taught that he came to be the servant of all. They thought that God's ruler would rely on force of arms. Jesus taught that he would win hearts by force of love. There are many such contrasts. Follow some of them through for yourself. But it is clear that Jesus believed that he was fulfilling the destiny which Israel had failed to achieve, modelling both God's perfect ruler and God's obedient servant. Many of his sayings indicate that the kingdom had already arrived with him: he was what one of the church fathers called 'the kingdom in himself'. He embodied it. He drew his followers into it. And so they were a sort of advance guard of the kingdom of God.

But Jesus never imagined they were the whole thing. There are many sayings of Jesus which show he knew a long time would elapse before the kingdom which he inaugurated would be consummated. That would happen at the end of time, at judgment day. A strong line of teaching throughout the New Testament insists that the world has not seen the last of Jesus Christ. He came in obscurity two thousand years ago. He will return in glory at the end of time. That is the Christian hope. He taught us in the Lord's Prayer to pray that God's will would one day be done on earth as it is in heaven. That day has not yet dawned. There is an 'already' and a 'not yet' about the kingdom of God. It has been introduced, but it has not been brought to fulfilment. One day it will be. That is the hope which

Christians have cherished ever since the resurrection. And the resurrection is the assurance in the midst of time that our hope about the end is not misplaced.

If that is, in sketchiest outline, the teaching of Jesus about the kingdom of God, where does the church fit in? That is a question to which there are several wrong answers!

One wrong answer *identifies the church with the kingdom*. God forbid! If the totality of the kingdom of God were no better than the poor old fallible church, I think I would opt out. No, the kingdom of God is a lot greater than the church. It includes heaven.

A second wrong answer *wants the kingdom without the king*. It is a sort of liberal humanism which majors on political and social issues. It relies on human beings to usher in the kingdom. It is a Utopian hope, and as such is doomed to failure. How can fallible, corrupt human beings bring in a perfect kingdom? It cannot be done.

A third wrong answer *wants the king without the kingdom*. It has a warm, personal and rather pious trust in Jesus as Saviour and Lord, but it sees no need to get involved in trying to sort this world out, because this world is going to pass away. Getting people to heaven is all that matters. This sort of pietism is very alien to the attitude of Jesus. Nobody would have thought of crucifying a pious mystic.

What then is the true relationship between the church and the kingdom? Surely something like this. God's 'kingdom' is not a place. It means his standing claim for allegiance on his rebel world. He is king, whether people acknowledge it or not. 'The Lord reigns' is one of the great themes of the whole Bible. So the kingdom of God is much bigger than the church. It includes every attitude, every kind deed, every true and honest endeavour wherever you may find them in the world. Those are God's ways, aspects of the way things are done when he is king. The church should rejoice whenever it sees goodness and love, integrity and generosity. These are kingdom values, and they are often shown in the lives of people who are not Christians, for a very good reason: all people are made in God's image, and although that image is marred in all of us it is not totally erased in any of us. So we should never be surprised to acknowledge virtue in an atheist or, for that matter, wickedness in a Christian.

The distinctive thing about the church lies not in having a monopoly on virtue but in being the only sphere within God's kingly rule that consciously acknowledges his sovereignty and seeks to obey it. And God has a great job for his church. It is both to embody the life and values of the kingdom and to try to win back God's rebel subjects into that service which is perfect freedom, the service of the king of kings. What a thrilling goal for our lives – to march by a different drum from secular society, and to call people to come and join the banner of the Lord Jesus Christ.

Will you consciously aim to live by kingdom values?

Will you welcome them wherever you find them?

Will you try to introduce other people to the Lord of the church?

Be careful. If you can say a humble 'yes' to those questions you are in danger of losing your 'amateur' churchgoing status!